Flowering shrubs
in cross-stitch

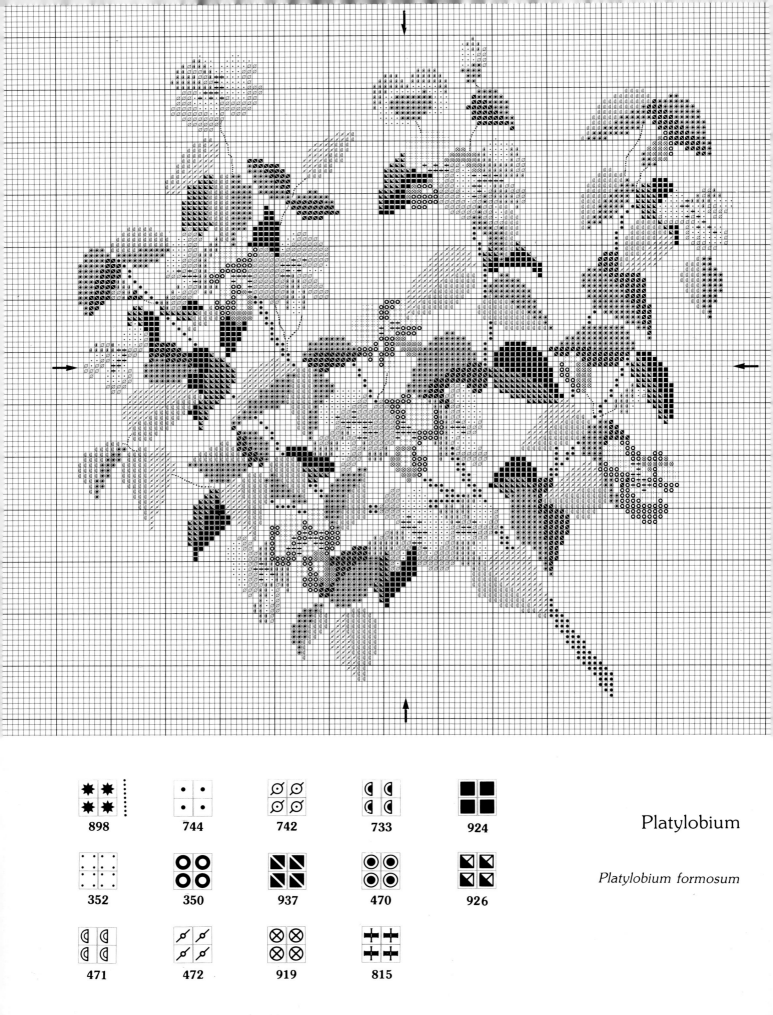

Flowering shrubs
in cross-stitch

ZARZA

LE TEMPS APPRIVOISÉ
7, rue Abel Hovelacque
75013 PARIS

Zarza

Zarza graduated in 1972 from the French school of industrial design, the Ecole nationale des arts appliqués à l'industrie, then studied for two years at the major French art school, the Ecole des Beaux-Arts.

A lover of nature and the countryside, he soon became known for his original compositions (Salon des ateliers d'art Exhibition, 1985).

He loves to experiment and is as skilled in airbrushing as in painting on silk.

Embroidery photographs: Janine Sicart.

Computerised diagrams: Jean-Claude Moissinac for Daikiri.

DMC has very efficiently helped us with the realisation of the embroideries

© Pierre Zech Éditeur, Paris, 1989
ISBN 2.283.58087.0
Printed in Spain

Introduction

From painting to embroidery...

Nature will always be a privileged and inexhaustible supply of inspiration for all art forms. The trained eye of the painter never ceases to discover its wonders. That is why all the patterns presented in this booklet were originally created in gouache paint.

The fine detailing and richness of colour, drawing and composition are remarkably well-adapted to the cross-stitch technique. The artist himself chose the correct DMC threads from the vast range of colours to match the hues indicated for each plant.

The practical advice at the beginning, which should be read before you begin work, makes these patterns suitable for all levels of embroiderers despite their apparent complexity.

Before you begin

The materials

The patterns shown here should be embroidered on evenweave linen of 10.5 threads to the centimeter (about 26 to the inch). The designs should be embroidered using two strands of DMC Mouliné Special (Ref.: art. 117) and a blunt-ended tapestry needle (number 22 to 24). An embroidery hoop is very useful to keep the fabric taut.

Using the diagrams

Each cross-stitch corresponds to one square of the diagram and covers two weft and two warp threads. The size of the finished embroidery thus depends on the number of threads per centimeter of the fabric used.
The symbols below each diagram correspond to the colours of thread used in the pattern. The number accompanying each symbol refers to the DMC colour chart which you will find on pages 10 and 11.

Preparing your work

Before starting to embroider, oversew the fabric all round to prevent it from unravelling. Then mark it out with tacking stitch in coloured thread, 1 inch from the edges, covering 10 threads over and 10 threads under the fabric on at least two sides. This will eventually help you to count your stitches. Then count the number of threads lengthwise and crosswise, and mark the halfway point, horizontally and vertically, with a row of running stitches in coloured thread (10 threads over and 10 threads under). The point at which the threads cross will give you the centre point, which is indicated on the diagrams by two arrows. Pull the running stitch out when the embroidery is completed.

Embroidery

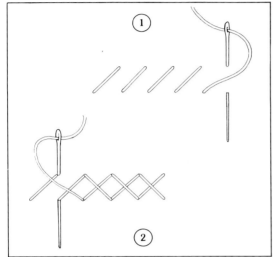

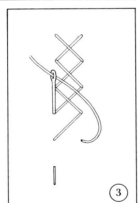

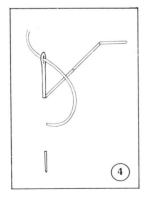

Cross-stitch
Each complete stitch consists of two diagonals which cross in the centre. To make a row of stitches, sew a series of diagonals, each covering two threads of the fabric working form bottom to top and from left to right (1), then go back over the stitches, using another series of diagonal stitches from right to left to cross over the previous series (2).
Begin at the top row.

To work vertically (3), each whole stitch must be completed separately. Sew a diagonal stitch from bottom to top and from left to right, then from right to left, bringing the needle out two threads below the stitch thus created, in order to begin the next one.

Whether you are working horizontally or vertically, all the stitches must cross in the same direction. It is also important for the neatness of the work not to pull the embroidery thread too tightly; the thread should cross two fabric threads without pulling them together.

Backstitch (4) is used for the stems. It forms a continuous line of short stitches which means you can follow curved lines. Insert the needle at the beginning of the line and bring it out a little further on. Bring the needle back and put it through the first hole, bringing it out a little further on, and so on.

Backstitch is shown on the diagrams by a full or dotted line repeated on the right of the symbol of the color to be used.

Try and avoid making knots when starting or finishing work. Leave a 1 1/5 inch (3 cm) end when you start the embroidery and hold it in place with subsequent stitches. To finish off or when a piece of thread is used up, slide the thread under the last stitches you made.

Needlework projects

The designs presented in the following pages will blend in beautifully with any colour scheme, thanks to their diversity of composition and colour. They will give your table linen an elegant, personalized note, or you can make them into various types of soft furnishings such as cushions, picture frames and so on.

Table runner
Fabric size: 15 × 41 inches (37 × 102 cm).
Size of finished needlework: 14 × 40 inches (35 × 100 cm).
First, center the chosen design on the fabric (the center of the embroidery should be about 7 1/2 inches (18,5 cm) from the edge of the fabric) at each end of the table runner. Finish with a 1/5 inch (5 cm) wide open hem made by pulling out two threads right around the needlework 2/3 inch (1,5 cm) from the edge.

Table linen set
Fabric size: 13 × 19 inches (32 × 47 cm).
Size of finished needlework: 12 × 18 inches (30 × 45 cm).
Proceed as for table runner.

Cushion
Fabric size: 17 × 34 1/2 inches (42 × 85 cm) for a 16 × 16 inches (40 × 40 cm) cushion.
Complete the embroidery, centering it on one half of the fabric. Assemble the cushion with backstitch, adding coloured piping if desired.

Framing
Fabric size: 18 × 18 inches (45 × 45 cm).
Frame the finished needlework with a passe-partout in a colour of your choice.

Needlework holder (not shown)
Fabric size: 18 1/2 × 26 inches (46 × 65 cm).
Size of the finished holder: 18 × 12 inches (44 × 30 cm).
Center the design within a rectangle made from half of the fabric. When you have completed the embroidery, assemble the holder using backstitch and line it with cotton fabric. If you like, you can add a zip fastner to close it. Then sew on the handles.

TABLEAU DE RECHERCHE DES Nos DE COULEURS
KEY TO COLOR NUMBERS
TABELLE ZUM AUFSUCHEN DER FARBNUMMERN
DMC KLEURENSCHEMA

Coul. Nos Color # Kleuren Nrs Farben	Col. Kolom	Coul. Nos Color # Kleuren Nrs Farben	Col. Kolom	Coul. Nos Color # Kleuren Nrs Farben	Col. Kolom	Coul. Nos Color # Kleuren Nrs Farben	Col. Kolom	Coul. Nos Color # Kleuren Nrs Farben	Col. Kolom	Coul. Nos Color # Kleuren Nrs Farben	Col. Kolom	Coul. Nos Color # Kleuren Nrs Farben	Col. Kolom	Coul. Nos Color # Kleuren Nrs Farben	Col. Kolom
Couleurs Ombrées		+ 301	3	452	17	+ 666	5	+ 798	7	+ 913	6	+ 995	12		
48	22	304	8	453	17	+ 676	14	+ 799	7	+ 915	7	+ 996	12		
51	20	+ 307	5	+ 469	12	+ 677	14	+ 800	7	917	7	3011	14		
52	21	+ 309	1	+ 470	12	680	14	+ 801	10	+ 918	11	3012	14		
53	21	+ 310	8	+ 471	12	+ 699	8	+ 806	11	919	11	3013	14		
57	20	311	3	+ 472	12	+ 700	8	+ 807	11	+ 920	11	3021	16		
61	21	312	3	+ 498	8	+ 701	8	809	7	921	11	3022	16		
62	22	315	13	500	15	+ 702	8	813	5	+ 922	11	3023	16		
67	22	316	13	+ 501	15	+ 703	8	814	8	924	15	3024	16		
69	20	317	12	+ 502	15	704	8	+ 815	8	926	15	3031	16		
75	21	+ 318	12	503	15	+ 712	3	816	8	927	15	3032	16		
90	20	319	1	+ 504	15	+ 718	7	817	5	928	15	3033	16		
91	21	+ 320	1	517	10	720	18	+ 818	1	+ 930	4	3041	16		
92	20	+ 321	8	+ 518	10	721	18	819	1	931	4	3042	16		
93	20	+ 322	3	+ 519	10	722	18	820	7	+ 932	4	+ 3045	13		
94	21	326	1	520	18	+ 725	7	+ 822	2	934	15	+ 3046	13		
95	20	327	16	522	18	+ 726	7	+ 823	3	935	12	3047	13		
99	21	333	18	523	18	+ 727	7	824	5	936	15	3051	15		
101	21	334	3	524	18	+ 729	14	825	5	+ 937	12	3052	15		
102	21	335	1	535	12	+ 730	14	+ 826	5	+ 938	10	3053	15		
103	20	+ 336	3	543	13	731	14	+ 827	5	939	3	3064	13		
104	22	340	18	550	8	+ 732	14	+ 828	5	+ 943	10	3072	17		
105	20	341	18	+ 552	8	733	14	+ 829	14	+ 945	9	3078	13		
106	21	347	11	+ 553	8	+ 734	14	830	14	946	1	+ 3325	3		
107	21	+ 349	5	+ 554	8	+ 738	10	831	14	+ 947	1	3326	1		
108	20	350	5	561	18	+ 739	10	+ 832	14	+ 948	5	3328	11		
111	22	+ 351	5	562	18	+ 740	2	833	14	+ 950	13	3340	19		
112	22	+ 352	5	563	18	741	2	+ 834	14	+ 951	13	3341	19		
113	20	+ 353	5	564	18	+ 742	2	+ 838	6	954	6	+ 3345	9		
114	22	355	9	+ 580	11	743	2	839	6	+ 955	6	3346	9		
115	22	+ 356	9	+ 581	11	+ 744	2	+ 840	6	+ 956	10	+ 3347	9		
116	22	367	1	+ 597	15	+ 745	2	+ 841	6	+ 957	10	+ 3348	9		
121	22	+ 368	1	+ 598	15	746	13	+ 842	6	958	19	3350	4		
122	22	369	1	600	6	+ 747	10	844	16	959	19	3354	4		
123	22	370	18	+ 601	6	+ 754	5	869	15	961	4	3362	19		
124	21	371	18	602	6	+ 758	9	+ 890	1	962	4	3363	19		
125	20	372	18	+ 603	6	760	11	891	2	963	4	3364	19		
126	22	400	3	604	6	761	11	+ 892	2	964	19	3371	10		
		+ 402	3	+ 605	6	+ 762	12	893	2	966	7	3607	19		
Couleurs Unies, Tapisserie et Nouv. Coloris		+ 407	13	+ 606	4	772	18	+ 894	2	970	9	3608	19		
		+ 413	12	+ 608	4	775	3	895	9	+ 971	9	3609	19		
		+ 414	12	610	16	+ 776	1	+ 898	10	+ 972	9	+ 3685	4		
‡*Bl. Neige	1	+ 415	12	611	16	778	13	+ 899	1	+ 973	9	+ 3687	4		
* Ecru	11	420	15	612	16	+ 780	7	+ 900	1	+ 975	12	3688	4		
+ 208	2	422	11	613	9	781	7	+ 902	8	+ 976	12	+ 3689	4		
209	2	+ 433	10	632	13	+ 782	7	+ 904	4	+ 977	12	3705	19		
+ 210	2	+ 434	10	‡ 640	2	+ 783	7	+ 905	4	986	3	3706	19		
+ 211	2	435	10	‡ 642	2	791	9	906	4	+ 987	3	3708	19		
221	13	+ 436	10	‡ 644	2	792	9	+ 907	4	988	3				
223	13	+ 437	10	645	16	793	9	+ 909	6	+ 989	3				
224	13	+ 444	5	646	16	794	9	910	6	+ 991	11				
225	13	+ 445	5	647	16	+ 796	7	+ 911	6	992	11				
+ 300	3	451	17	648	16	+ 797	7	912	6	+ 993	11				

DMC COLOR CHART
(Art. 117-115-116)

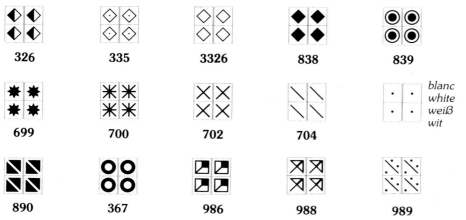

326	335	3326	838	839
699	700	702	704	blanc / white / weiß / wit
890	367	986	988	989

Garland flower

Daphne cneorum

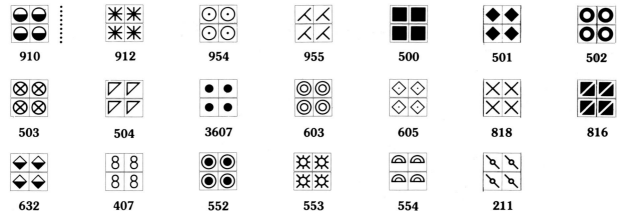

Dog-rose bush

Rosa canina

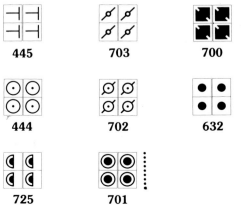

Ribbed melilot

Melilotus officinalis

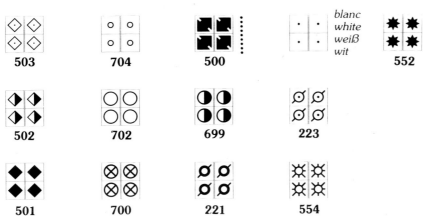

Mentastrum

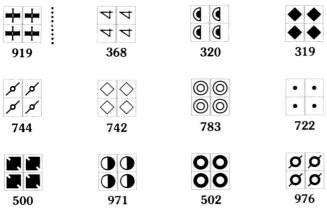

Laburnum

Laburnum anagyroides

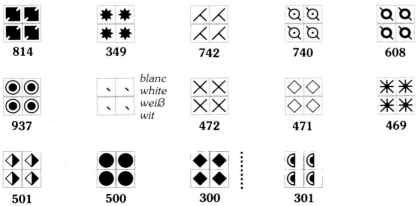

Firethorn

Pyracantha coccinea

Wood sanicle

Sanicula europaea

Valerian

Valeriana officinalis

27

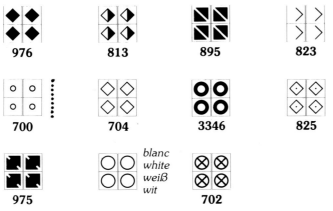

Lemon tree

Citrus limonium

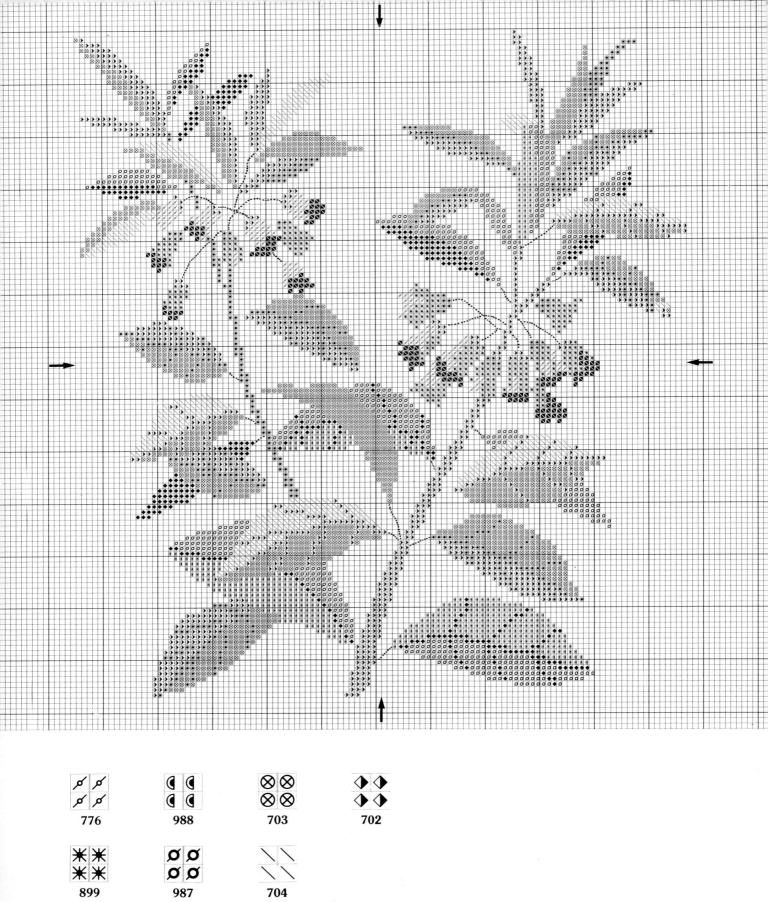

Enkianthus

Enkianthus campanulatus

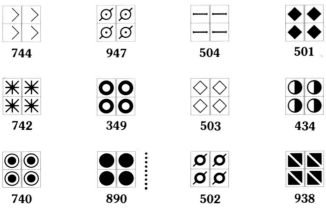

Barberry

Berberis vulgaris

33

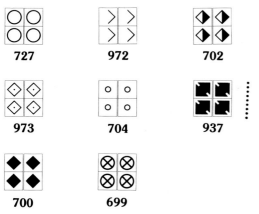

St. John's wort

Hypericum perforatum

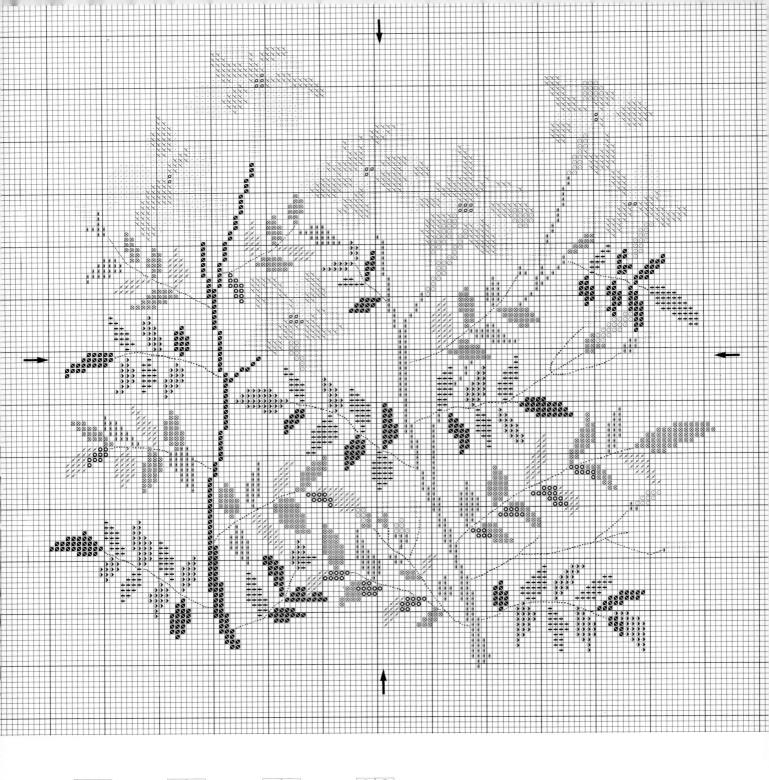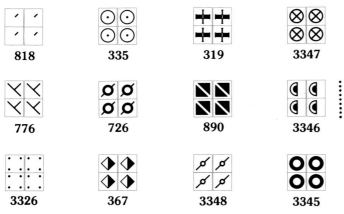

Jasmin

Jasminum

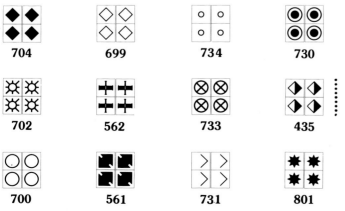

Bay willow

Salix pentendra

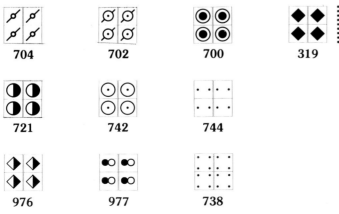

Solanum capsicastrum

Bog myrtle

Myrica gale

Lady's mantle

Alchemilla vulgaris

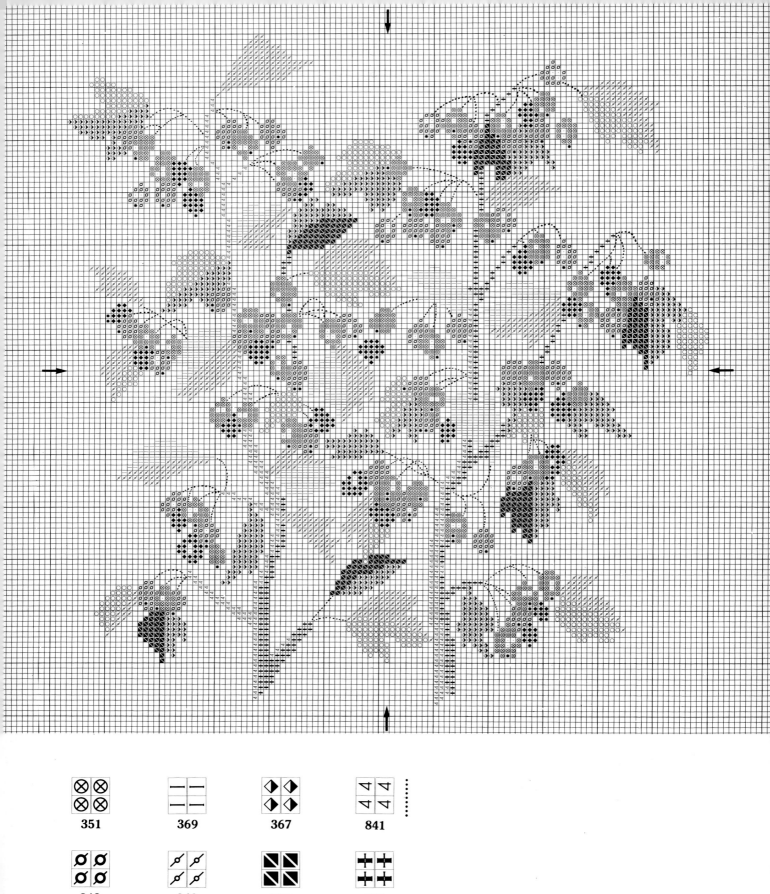

Hawthorn

Crataegus laevigata

47

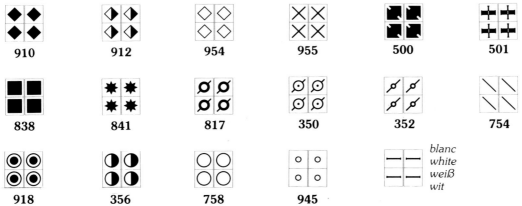

Quince

Cydonia oblonga

49

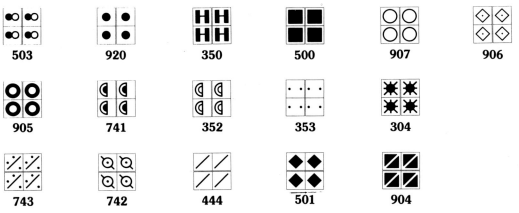

Jacaranda

Bignonia capensis

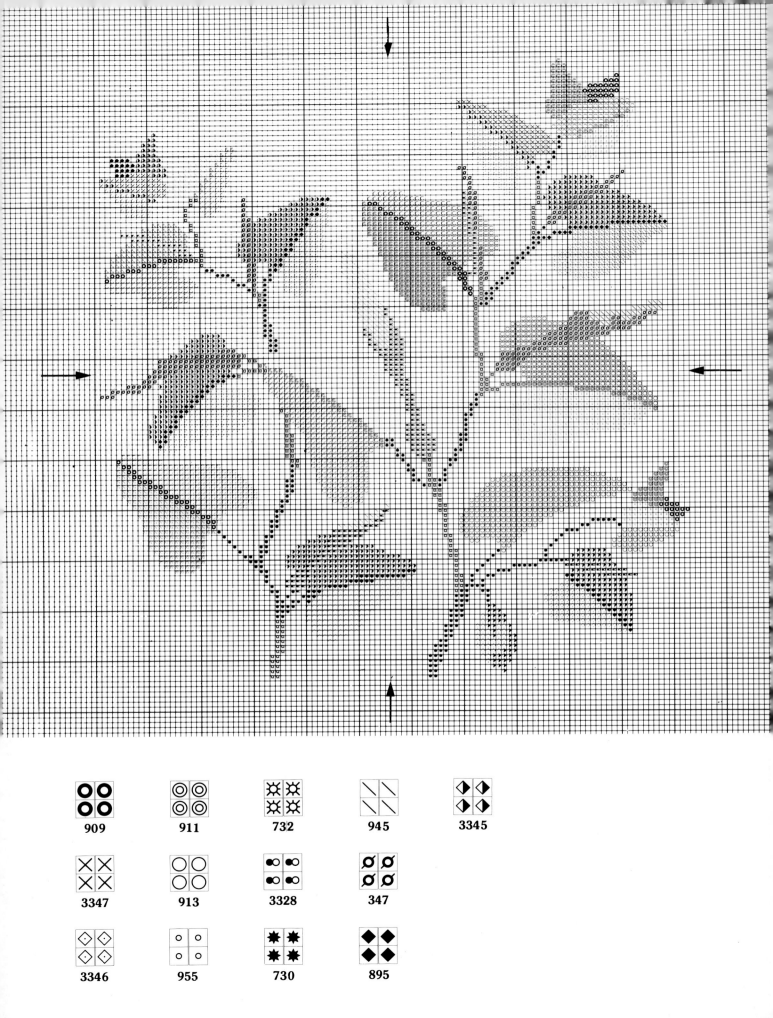

Calico flower

Aristolochia elegans

Thalictrum aquilegifolium

Kumquat

57

Spiraea vanhouttei

Arbutus

Arbutus uva-ursi